BOYS, GIRLS, AND OTHER MYTHOLOGICAL CREATURES

Boys, Girls, and Other Mythological Creatures

A Play for Young Audiences

Mark Crawford

Boys, Girls, and Other Mythological Creatures
first published 2018 by Scirocco Drama
An imprint of J. Gordon Shillingford Publishing Inc.

Scirocco Drama Editor: Glenda MacFarlane

Cover artwork and design by Doowah Design

Author photo by Liz Beddall
Production photos by Lauren Garbutt

Printed and bound in Canada on 100% post-consumer recycled paper.
We acknowledge the financial support of the Manitoba Arts Council and The Canada Council for the Arts for our publishing program.

Licensing inquiries, please contact:

Colin Rivers, Marquis Entertainment
312-73 Richmond Street West
Toronto, ON M5H 4E8
info@mqlit.ca
416.960.9123

Library and Archives Canada Cataloguing in Publication

Crawford, Mark, 1981-, author
Boys, girls, and other mythological creatures : a play for young audiences / Mark Crawford.

ISBN 978-1-927922-43-9 (softcover)

I. Title.

PS8605.R435B69 2018 jC812'.6 C2018-904259-1

J. Gordon Shillingford Publishing
P.O. Box 86, RPO Corydon Avenue, Winnipeg, MB Canada R3M 3S3

For boys, girls, and other mythological creatures everywhere.

Mark Crawford

Mark Crawford is an actor and playwright. His plays *Stag and Doe, Bed and Breakfast,* and *The Birds and the Bees* are published by Scirocco Drama. All three of these plays have received productions from coast to coast. His latest play, *The New Canadian Curling Club,* premiered at the Blyth Festival in 2018. As an actor, Mark has performed with theatre companies across Canada. He grew up on his family's farm near Glencoe, Ontario, and he now lives in Stratford.

Acknowledgements

I would like to acknowledge The Cabaret Company, Carousel Players, Roseneath Theatre, Theatre Direct Canada, and Young People's Theatre for their recommendations of funding through the Ontario Arts Council's Theatre Creators' Reserve. Thank you!

For their tremendous contributions to this play, thank you to Jessica Carmichael, the cast, and creative team of the premiere production. For their hard work and unwavering belief in the play, thanks to the staff of Carousel Players. At the time of the premiere, they were: Jane Gardner, General Manager; Lauren Hundert, Outreach and Marketing Manager; Kate Leathers, Production Manager. For their steadfast support, thanks to Carousel Players' Board of Directors: Jenniffer Anand, Sande Farrauto, Sarah Lynch, Carolyn Mackenzie, Corey Miles, Paddy Parr, Keith Tait, and Dave Thomas.

Big thanks to: Brian Dudkiewicz, Sam Ferguson, Cynthia Jimenez-Hicks, Jesse LaVercombe, Matt Pilipiak, and Edmund Stapleton for their participation in play development workshops; Ontario Power Generation for their financial support of the Carousel production; Stephanie Vail, Quest Community Health, and Rainbow Niagara for their help during rehearsals and public performances; Enzo DeDivitiis and Pride Niagara for their allyship at our community presentation; Reverend Bill Thomas and our friends at Silver Spire United Church; the staff of the Toronto Public Library, particularly the Bloor-Gladstone branch; my agent Colin Rivers and the team at Marquis Literary; Monica Dufault and Essential Collective Theatre; The Marilyn I. Walker School of Fine and Performing Arts – Brock University; Pablo Felices-Luna and Manitoba Theatre for Young People; Andrew Lamb and Roseneath Theatre; David Nairn, Sharyn Ayliffe, and Theatre Orangeville; Lynda Hill and Theatre Direct Canada for hosting the Carousel production in Toronto; Karen Fricker for her foreword; Glenda MacFarlane and Karen Haughian at Scirocco Drama for their continued support of my work; Paul Dunn for his love, patience, and encouragement; and all of the folks I talked to in my research for this play – the grown-ups, the parents, the teachers, and most importantly, the kids.

We remember the late Debra McLauchlan and her incredible passion for theatre for young audiences and Carousel Players. Debra, your grandkids were some of the first children to see this play. I think they liked it!

During the first run of *Boys, Girls, and Other Mythological Creatures,* some people didn't take kindly to the idea of kids watching this play. I am very grateful for everyone who supported me, the play, and our production at that time. Most of all, I thank the young audiences. They responded to the play with open hearts and open minds and helped put everything into perspective. In the words of Simone: "Thank you for your help with the candles."

Foreword

by Karen Fricker

"*That* Mark Crawford?"

This was my reaction in the early spring of 2017 when I saw that Carousel Players, the venerable theatre company for young audiences based in St. Catharines, Ontario was producing the world premiere of Crawford's play *Boys, Girls, and Other Mythological Creatures*.

Only a few months earlier I'd seen Crawford's work as an actor for the first time in Groundling Theatre's productions of *A Winter's Tale* and *Measure for Measure*. His extraordinary skill with Shakespeare's language, his capacity to bring out the gentle humanity in his comic characters, and the generosity of his engagement with the other performers were some of those productions' most memorable elements.

As he performs, so he writes: these qualities of gentleness, close attention to language, and sensitivity to the complexity of human interaction are everywhere on display in this, his first play for young audiences.

In an interview for a *Toronto Star* column, Crawford told me that the idea for *Boys, Girls…* came to him while performing in schools as an actor in previous Carousel Players productions:

"I would see these kids, getting on the bus or getting picked up from school, who weren't fitting into what we typically call boy and girl. They weren't locked into that binary… I would just wonder a lot. What is that existence, who are those kids, who are they going to become?"

Such observations grew into this play about eight-year-old Simon, who sees an audience waiting to be "wowed" where other people see blank walls and empty spaces. Simon and his classmate Abby are working together on a school project to create a fairy tale, and she is planning to write down a story. Simon has another idea: "Our fairy tale should be a play. Don't worry – I'm an expert."

For Simon's thirteen-year-old brother Zach, however, this love of playacting is not "normal." Nor is Simon's love of the colour purple and Barbie dolls. As Simon and Abby devise their tale about how to be your "True Self," contending throughout with her worries about being laughed at by their peers, Zach gets drawn into their imaginative universe, and the family basement becomes an enchanted world, complete with a dragon named Illuminauticus.

Along the way, Simon self-reinvents as the fairy tale heroine, Princess Simone, and in this guise finds the power to save Abigail from captivity at the hands of King Zachariah.

At no point in Crawford's script is the concept of transgender identity directly articulated, and the end of the play is indeterminate:

ZACH: So if this is like... your true self and everything, does that mean you're gonna be a girl all the time? Like, instead of being my brother, are you my sister now or something?

SIMON(E): I'm not sure.... Maybe. Maybe not.

This is what I mean by gentleness: in the play Simon(e) explores their gender identity in a playful, "what if" context without coming to any definite conclusions. The character who goes on the biggest personal journey in the play is not Simon(e) but Zach, who learns to accept his younger sibling on their own terms.

Carousel's production, developed and directed by its then-artistic director Jessica Carmichael, was geared for audiences of six-to-ten-year-olds, in keeping with the 2015 Ontario Health and Physical Education curriculum which teaches early year students about gender identity and expression. It played to twenty-two elementary schools in the Niagara/Hamilton region in April 2017. When I saw it performed at CH Norton

Public School in Burlington, nearly every child in the audience shot their hand in the air when the cast asked if it's okay for anyone to play with dolls or trucks.

Response to the production then turned less than gentle: five schools in the Niagara Catholic District School Board (NCDSB) cancelled their bookings for the play in quick succession, in response to concerns raised by a superintendent that it was not appropriate for a primary school audience. In a controversy that reached the national media, Carmichael raised concerns that the cancellations were based on misinformation and reflected fear and intolerance, while the NCDSB maintained that the play's themes were unsuitable for the youngest audience members in the prescribed age range.

In an interview with the *Niagara Falls Review*, Carmichael pointed to the irony that this story about acceptance was having difficulty being accepted: "I believe gender non-conforming kids exist, and their stories matter. I want to live in a world where their stories can be shared and celebrated. I want these kids to know we see them. They are not alone."

The cancelled performances affected Carousel's bottom line, but the controversy had the positive effect of raising awareness about the play and its themes, and two additional public performances – one in St. Catharines and another in Toronto – were added in response to community interest. The organization's board reported "overwhelming encouragement and appreciation from stakeholders, supporters and strangers" in the wake of cancellations, saying that amongst the many individuals and organizations which had contacted them were people who had never seen the company's work but nonetheless "thanked us for presenting a play about freedom of choice."

In an open letter responding to the cancellations, Crawford acknowledged that the experience had shaken him, and that he wished he could be "as fierce and fearless" as Princess Simone. "I'm frightened by people who want to limit children's access to art, theatre, beauty, magic, joy, humour, and big ideas," he wrote. "I'm frightened by statistics that show LGBTQ kids commit suicide at much higher rates than straight kids – not because they are disordered or broken, but because they live in a society that continues to tell them they are not worthy."

Live theatre by its nature disappears, but the publication of this script makes the play available to a broad public, and could lead to further productions down the line. More Simon(e)s, Abbys, and Zachs could see themselves onstage as a result, and come closer to accepting their True Selves. And that's nothing to be afraid of.

Karen Fricker is a freelance theatre critic for The Toronto Star *and an Assistant Professor of Dramatic Arts at Brock University. She is a member of the Canadian Theatre Critics Association, the Toronto Theatre Critics Awards, and the Canadian Association for Theatre Research. Originally from Los Angeles, she has reviewed theatre in New York, L.A., Dublin, and London.*

Production History

Boys, Girls, and Other Mythological Creatures was first produced by Carousel Players. This production toured to schools and theatres in April and May, 2017 with the following cast:

SIMON..................................Matt Pilipiak
ABBY ....Cynthia Jimenez-Hicks
ZACH ....Drew O'Hara

The premiere production was dramaturged and directed by Jessica Carmichael.

Set and costume design – Brian Dudkiewicz

Sound design – Sam Ferguson

Stage Manager – JoAnna Black

Production Manager – Kate Leathers

Mask and puppet design – Clelia Scala

Characters

Simon, 8

Abby, 8

Zach, 13

Setting

We are in a basement. It's unfinished; chances are, it's not even dry-walled—just concrete block. We can see the stairs coming down—a whole staircase an entire storey high; if that's not possible, a few steps will do just fine. These stairs lead to the main floor of this house and they are the only real way in and out of here.

In this basement, there are boxes, plastic bins, some labelled, some not. There is a box of dress-up clothes, an old toy box. There might be a stepladder, a shelving unit, an ironing board, an old lamp or two, and some Christmas decorations. There is a clothesline or drying rack on which hangs an adult woman's dress. If possible, there is a bare light bulb hanging overhead which the characters can turn on or off to make it light or dark. Most of the stuff we see in the play comes from within this very regular, slightly messy family basement. It doesn't need to be a completely realistic set, but off the top of the show, there is certainly nothing magical about it. That takes us by surprise…

This basement is also a theatre. It's also a castle, a courtyard, a moat, a forest, a drawbridge, a Tower of Light, and many other locations.

The Audience lives in the walls of this basement. They are there when we need them.

Time

A spring afternoon in the present. And a long, long time ago.

A Few Notes from the Playwright

In an effort to allow directors, designers, and actors to create their own unique productions, I've tried to keep the stage directions to a minimum. I encourage you to bring all of the moments and images to life in creative, playful ways. In my mind, there is no such thing as narration in this script. Keep it active and have fun.

I've tried to capture the rhythm of kids making up a story as they go along. There are a lot of ellipses in this text. Don't think of them pauses; think of them as the search for the right word or…the active thought before making an offer for the next moment in the story.

In an attempt to reflect Simon's journey, I've made some choices for the character's name and pronouns in this published text. Feel free use these details as clues in rehearsal, but keep in mind, the language we use for gender is imperfect and ever-evolving.

Darkness.

From upstairs, we hear the front door open and close. Footsteps. And then SIMON's voice getting closer…

SIMON: Come on in! This way! Follow me.

SIMON enters, followed by ABBY. They both have backpacks. SIMON flicks on the light.

Riiiiight down heeeere! Oh – watch your step. So! Here we are. I thought we could do our work down here. Welcome!

ABBY: Uhhh…thanks.

SIMON: So. I think our story should begin: (*Trumpet call.*) Bah-bah-bah-BAAAH! "Once Upon a Time!"

ABBY: Umm…

SIMON: "Long, long ago…"

ABBY: Let me just get my notebook. (*She pulls it out of her backpack.*)

SIMON: "In a giant castle far, far away…"

ABBY: Let me write this down.

SIMON: "There lived a…" "There lived a…" Who do you want your character to be?

ABBY: My character? What do you mean "my character"?

SIMON: Well, I had this great idea that we could do our story as…A PLAY!

ABBY: Pardon?

SIMON: A play, Abby. When we present our fairy tale for the class tomorrow, we should do it as a play.

ABBY: Um, Simon? (*Referring to the work sheet.*) The assignment is for everyone to come up with their own fairy tale, write it down, and just… read it in front of the class.

SIMON: Well, sure, that's the assignment. But we're special; we get to be partners.

ABBY: Yeah. Right. Ms. da Silva said I should work with you.

SIMON: I know! Isn't that great?! This way, you don't have to do a presentation in front of the class all by yourself in your first week at a new school.

ABBY: …Exactly.

SIMON: But also, Ms. da Silva knows I'm sooo good at presentations. Which is why our fairy tale should be a play! Don't worry – I'm an expert. This is where I make up all of my plays. Here, in my basement. See? This…is my stage.

ABBY: OK.

SIMON: And this right here…I sometimes use as a curtain.

ABBY: Uh huh.

SIMON: And I have all this stuff down here we can use. This stuff here and all this stuff over here. And even this weird thing here. And I have this whole box of costumes. And this – this is the most important part.

ABBY: What?

SIMON: The Audience.

ABBY: Pardon?

SIMON: The Audience, Abby! Hello, Audience! Don't you see them?

ABBY: Uhhh, no. The thing is? When we do our story in front of the class? I really, really don't want to look…weird.

SIMON: …Oh.

ABBY: I've only been at our school for four days. Our class doesn't even know me.

SIMON: So this is their chance to get to know you.

ABBY: If you think it'll work.

SIMON: Of course it'll work! The Audience is going to love you. So! Fairy tale! Bah-bah-bah BAAAH!!! Once upon a time, long, long ago, in a giant castle far, far away, there lived a…

ABBY: (*Casting SIMON's role instead of her own.*) A… young prince.

SIMON: Prince…Simon! (*He throws on a cape or other costume piece. It's purple.*) TA-DA!

We hear the front door again and a voice from up above. SIMON stops dead.

ZACH: SIMON!?!

SIMON: Yeah?

ZACH: DID YOU WALK HOME ALL BY YOURSELF!?

SIMON: Uhhh… NO! (*To ABBY.*) That's Zach – my big brother. Ever since he turned thirteen, we're allowed to be home alone till my mom and dad get home from work, but I'm not supposed to walk home by myself.

ZACH enters on the stairs.

ZACH: I was waiting for you by the door at school, Simon. I didn't even know where you were! (*He sees ABBY.*) Who the heck are you?

SIMON: This is my friend. Abby.

ZACH: You have a friend?

SIMON: Yes.

ZACH: Why does your friend have to be a girl?

SIMON: Um –

ZACH: What the heck are you wearing?

SIMON: Oh, this is just a –

ZACH: Please tell me you didn't wear that at school.

SIMON: Well, no, it's just –

ZACH: Purple. Why do you always want everything to be purple?

SIMON: I don't know, it's my favourite –

ZACH: Did Mom and Dad say you're allowed to have someone over?

SIMON: We're working on a presentation. For school.

ZACH: Why are you doing it in the basement? (*To ABBY.*) There's mice down here, you know. (*Back to SIMON.*) What the heck is down here that you like so much?

SIMON looks to The Audience and shushes them.

What are you doing?

SIMON: Nothing.

ZACH: (*To ABBY.*) Do your parents know you're here?

ABBY: I told my sister; she texted my mom. It's okay because it's school work.

SIMON: Yeah, we're working, Zach. Can you leave us alone?

ZACH: Fine. But no getting into trouble. (*A private warning.*) You know what I'm talking about.

ZACH exits.

SIMON: Sorry. He used to be fun, but now he's…not. So: where were we?

ABBY: Uhhh…you're Prince Simon. (*Checking the sheet.*) Maybe that can be the protagonist. The main character.

SIMON: Yes! And Prince Simon has everything he wants: a huge bedroom painted purple; a pool in his backyard; ice cream or pizza or sushi any time he wants. And all the costumes in the world! A whole closet full of costumes!

ABBY: Buuut…

SIMON: But what?

ABBY: Well, there's no story if he's just this happy prince who has everything he wants. There has to be… (*Consults the sheet.*) Conflict.

SIMON: Oh. Right. Buuut...even though Prince Simon has all that stuff, he…he wishes he was something else.

ABBY: What does he wish he was?

SIMON: I don't know if I can tell you. The king, Prince Simon's father, is really mean and won't even let him say it.

ABBY writes this down.

But oh oh oh! I have an amazing idea for our play. I'll be right back!

Simon runs out. Maybe we can hear running up above. And immediately from off:

ZACH: SIMON! NO RUNNING IN THE HOUSE!

ABBY looks for The Audience again, but she can't see them. We hear a magical sound – almost from the distance. ABBY can't hear that either. ZACH reappears on the stairs.

What was your name again?

ABBY: Abby.

ZACH: And you're friends with my brother?

ABBY: Um, I guess?

ZACH: You guess?

ABBY: I'm new here. We just moved, my mom and my sister and me? Ms. da Silva paired me up with Simon so –

ZACH: You know he's not…normal, right?

ABBY: He's not?

ZACH: Haven't you noticed that he's kinda... different? From the other boys? He's always been weird, ever since he was really little, but lately, it has been getting way, way worse.

ABBY: What do you mean?

ZACH: Don't you see it? He acts like – Like, he's always pretending to be – He wishes he was a...

ABBY: A what?

ZACH: A girl.

SIMON appears on the stairs with something hidden in his shirt.

SIMON: Zach, I asked you to leave us alone.

ZACH: What's that?

SIMON: Nothing.

ZACH: What is in there?

SIMON: Nothing, okay? It's for our play.

ZACH: Your play? I thought it was a presentation.

SIMON: It is.

ZACH: Let me see it. (*He tries to get it and chases SIMON.*)

SIMON: ZACH!

ZACH: Let me see!

SIMON: It's nothing!

ZACH: Then show it to me!

They have a tussle. ZACH pulls the cape over SIMON's head.

SIMON: It's none of your business!

ZACH succeeds and gets it. It's a Barbie. Beat.

ZACH: What is this!?

SIMON: Um...

ZACH: Simon! What the heck is this?

ABBY: It looks like a Barbie.

ZACH: I know it looks like a Barbie! I can see it looks like a Barbie! Where in the heck did you get a Barbie?

SIMON: From my room?

ZACH: No! Where did you get it in the first place?

SIMON: I bought it! At Mr. Davidson's yard sale. I bought it when Dad wasn't looking. I bought it with my own money, so it's mine. (*He snatches it back.*)

ZACH: Mom and Dad don't know you have this?

SIMON: ...No.

ZACH: You'll be in so much trouble if they find out. You better not take it to school, Simon. You better not use it in your play, in front of your whole class? I mean, think about it. Think about what will happen.

ZACH leaves.

ABBY: What does he mean, "Think about what will happen"?

SIMON: Never mind.

ABBY: Oh. Well, I don't care that you have a Barbie.

SIMON: You don't?

ABBY: No. And I want to know your idea – for our fairy tale. You don't have to do it for the class if you don't want. Just...show me.

SIMON: ...It's late at night. And Prince Simon is in bed. I'm all alone and...I'm scared.

ABBY: How come?

SIMON: Because I wish I was something else, remember? But I'm not allowed to say it.

ABBY: Oh, right.

SIMON: But just like that! My fairy godmother (*Barbie*) comes in and puts a spell on me. Hey – you do this part.

ABBY: Uhhh... What's the spell?

SIMON: I don't know. Make it up.

ABBY: (*A reluctant puppeteer.*) Uhhh... "Prince Simon, I am your fairy godmother!"

SIMON: But maybe more of a fairy voice.

ABBY: Oh uh... (*She does a fairy voice.*) "Like this?"

SIMON: Yeah!

ABBY: "Prince Simon, it's me, your fairy godmother!"

SIMON: AHH!!!

ABBY: Sorry, did I scare you?

SIMON: Yeah, Fairy Godmother, but that's OK. I get scared really easily.

ABBY: "Not for long! I am here to give you magic powers!"

SIMON: What kind of magic powers?

ABBY: "Magic powers to…" umm…

SIMON: To transform.

ABBY: "Magic powers to transform! Into anything you wish!"

SIMON: Yes!

ABBY: "Buuut…"

SIMON: Why does there have to be a but? HA HA! Why does there have to be a BUTT!?

ABBY: This always happens in fairy tales. Like the fairy godmother gives Cinderella the big dress and the carriage to go to the ball, buuut it all disappears at midnight. So Prince Simon can transform…

ABBY & SIMON: Buuut…

SIMON: I can only transform…in the dark!

ABBY: "Prince Simon, you can only transform in the dark." Oh! Also: "There is one very special thing you were meant to be! That one very special thing is called…"

SIMON: My…true self.

ABBY: "Your True Self."

That magical sound again. Weird…did SIMON hear something?

Also! "Until you transform into Your True Self, you will always, always be afraid."

Simon (Matt Pilipiak) shows off Prince Simon's purple cape.

Abby (Cynthia Jimenez-Hicks) and Fairy Godmother Barbie put a spell on Simon (Matt Pilipiak).

SIMON: What? Abby!

ABBY: Trust me. This is really, really good for our story. Ms. da Silva will definitely give us extra marks for that. "Good luck, Simon! Good luck transforming into Your True Self!"

She gives Fairy Godmother Barbie a dramatic, magical exit.

SIMON: Wow. You know, you're pretty good at doing plays.

ABBY: I am?

SIMON: Yeah. I think The Audience likes you.

ABBY: (*She looks for them. Nothing.*) Huh. Now what?

SIMON: It's the middle of the night and Prince Simon sneaks out of his room, past the bedroom of the mean king, and into the courtyard. It's completely dark. I wish...I wish...I wish to be a...n elf.

ABBY: An elf? Do you think an elf is Your True Self?

SIMON: Who knows?

ABBY: So just like that, Prince Simon is transformed into an elf.

SIMON: Tiny in size. Little hat. (*He shrinks and finds something to wear as an elf hat.*)

ABBY: And a funny little elf voice.

SIMON: "I'm an elf. I'm an elf! Look at me, I'm an elf!"

ABBY: BOO!

SIMON: What are you doing?

ABBY: I'm trying to scare you to see if you're afraid. If you're not, then this is Your True Self.

SIMON: Oh! Got it. Try it again. "I'm an elf. I'm an elf! Look at me, I'm an elf!"

ABBY: BOO!

SIMON: AHH!

ABBY: AHH!

SIMON: AHHHHH! Wait. Why are you screaming?

ABBY: You scared me!

SIMON: No, you scared me! AHHHHH!!!!

ABBY & SIMON: AHHHHHHHH!!!!

ZACH comes bounding down the stairs.

ZACH: WHAT'S WRONG?

SIMON: Nothing.

ZACH: Then why are you screaming?

ABBY: Prince Simon was afraid.

ZACH: Prince Simon? What the heck are you wearing now?

SIMON: (*Taking off the elf hat.*) Nothing. Just leave us alone, Zach.

ZACH: What is this play even about?

ABBY: It's a fairy tale.

ZACH: A fairy tale!?

ABBY: That's the assignment. See? (*She holds up the sheet.*) Prince Simon can transform, but only in the dark.

ZACH: Whatever. No more screaming. And no more dressing up. Don't be such a – Urrrgh!

ZACH exits.

ABBY: It's okay. My sister doesn't get me either. So where were we? Right. You were scared. Which means an elf is not Your True Self. Then what?

SIMON: It's the next night and I sneak out of my room again. Past the big bad king.

ABBY: Back to the courtyard. Again, it's pitch black.

SIMON: And very quietly, so I don't get in trouble: I wish…I wish…I wish to be a…unicorn?

ABBY: A unicorn?

SIMON: Well, I like unicorns.

ABBY: Who doesn't? But is that the one thing you're really, really meant to be?

SIMON: One way to find out!

ABBY: So just like that, Prince Simon is transformed into a unicorn.

SIMON: (*Cobbling together a unicorn look.*) White hair, a long, flowing tail –

ABBY: And one beautiful golden horn.

SIMON: Oooohhh! "I'm a unicorn! I'm a unicorn! I'm a UUUUNICOOORN!"

ABBY: Ready?

SIMON: For what?

ABBY: THE UNICORN KILLER! (*She's found something to wear as the unicorn killer.*)

SIMON: AHHH!

ABBY: I'M GONNA GET YOUR HORN!

SIMON: NOOOOOO!!!

ABBY: I COLLECT UNICORN HORNS! THEY GIVE ME LIIIIIFE! I NEED YOUR HORN TO LIIIIIIVE!!!

SIMON & ABBY: AHHHHHHHHHHH!!!!!!

ZACH runs in again. But the unicorn killer (ABBY) rips the unicorn's horn off.

SIMON & ABBY: AHHHHHHHHHHH!!!!!!

ZACH: What did I say about screaming?!?

SIMON: Oops.

ABBY: Sorry.

ZACH: And what did I say about dressing up? What were you pretending to be this time?

ABBY: A unicorn.

SIMON: Abby!

ZACH: A unicorn, Simon? You're gonna dress up as a unicorn in front of your class? And run around like that? And scream like that? Aren't you afraid they'll laugh at you? Come on!

ZACH exits.

ABBY: What's wrong with unicorns?

SIMON: They're like…a girl thing. It doesn't matter anyway. A unicorn is not My True Self.

ABBY: Are they gonna laugh at us? Our class?

SIMON: Not if our play is amazing.

Beat.

ABBY: The next night. It's the darkest it's ever, ever been. So dark you can't even see one millimetre in front of you.

SIMON: I go back to the courtyard. Sneaking past the evil king.

ABBY: But it's so dark, you get lost on the way.

SIMON: What!

ABBY: Yeah, you get lost and…wander over to the castle's moat.

SIMON: The moat?! Eeeww! The moat is so gross and so scary. I know! I wish…I wish…I wish to be a…mermaid!

ABBY: A mermaid?

SIMON: Well, a mermaid can swim in the moat, so –

ABBY: Why don't you just say it? Say what you really wish to be.

SIMON: I can't! I will get in big trouble from the king, remember?

ABBY: Oh. (*She looks to the stairs.*) Yeah.

SIMON: So, all alone in the deep, dark moat –

ABBY: Prince Simon is transformed into a mermaid.

SIMON: (*Puts on a DIY mermaid outfit with ABBY's help.*) Ooooh! I love it!

ABBY: And the mermaid sings a mermaid song.

SIMON: A what?

ABBY: A mermaid song!

SIMON improvises a mermaid song.

But the mermaid's song wakes up the deadly sea creature that lives in the moat!

ABBY puppeteers something as the sea creature. SIMON continues to sing, now frightened.

And the deadly sea creature gets closer…

SIMON sings, scared!

And closer…

SIMON sings! Eeek!

And then it goes in for the attack!

SIMON: NOOOOOOOO!!! GET IT OFF ME! GET IT OFF ME! AHHHHHHH!!!!

ABBY & SIMON: AHHHHHHHHHH!!!!!

ZACH enters and sees SIMON as the mermaid, screaming and laughing and being attacked.

ZACH: What is that!?!

SIMON: Nothing! A mermaid, I mean no it's not, it was just in the dress-up box, I found it, Mom wore it once for Hallowe'en or no, it was Abby's, she brought it, I don't know!

ZACH: Why do you have it on?

SIMON: I don't!

Indeed, SIMON has removed the mermaid costume. ZACH picks up the sheet.

ZACH: Let me look at this.

SIMON: Zach, it's fine. We won't make any more noise. I promise.

ZACH: Fairy tale. Protagonist. Conflict. Antagonist. It doesn't say anything here about mermaids. It doesn't say anything about unicorns. It doesn't say anything about dressing up!

SIMON: We're just figuring it out.

ZACH: Yeah? Who's your protagonist then?

ABBY: Prince Simon.

ZACH: And what's your conflict?

ABBY: He wishes he was something else so he won't be afraid.

ZACH: What do you wish you were, Simon?

ABBY: He's not allowed to say it.

ZACH: How come?

SIMON: Prince Simon's dad, the very mean and very evil king, won't let him.

ZACH: So is he like…the antagonist?

SIMON: Sure. Now leave us alone.

ZACH: Who's playing the king?

SIMON: No one; he's not actually in the play.

ZACH: Well, he probably should be.

SIMON: No! Just go upstairs and watch TV.

ZACH: Maybe I should be the king.

SIMON: NO! This is for our class, Zach.

ZACH: But you two don't know what the heck you're doing. You need my help.

ABBY: No, really, we're fine.

ZACH: I'm stepping in! I'm here to help! I'm the king!

SIMON: You can't come to our class and do the presentation.

ZACH: You said you were figuring it out. I'll just help you…figure it out.

SIMON: Zach!

ZACH: I'll tell Mom and Dad about your Barbie. (*Beat.*) Okay. So why is this king so mean?

SIMON: He's just…a bad guy. That should be easy for you.

ZACH: I'm not a bad guy!

ABBY: Maybe…maybe he's so mean because…the queen died when Prince Simon was born and you blame him for her death.

SIMON: What?!

ABBY: You need a costume.

ZACH: No, no, no, I never said I would dress up.

ABBY: But how will The Audience know you're the king? Here.

She hands him some king costume pieces from the costume box. ZACH reluctantly puts them on.

ZACH: Awww yeeeah, I'm The King.

ABBY: But you should do a king voice.

SIMON: He can't. He's no good at doing plays.

ZACH: Yes I am! (*He attempts a king voice.*) I'm The King.

SIMON: See?

ABBY: Try it again, only lower.

ZACH: I am The King of this Whole Kingdom!

ABBY: And louder.

ZACH: And I am so mad because my beautiful queen is dead.

ABBY: And meaner.

ZACH: And it's all because of my miserable, terrible, awful son, PRINCE SIMON!

ABBY: Whoa.

ZACH finds his old toy bow and arrow.

ZACH: Now come on, Prince Simon: you're going to learn how to shoot this bow and arrow like a real man.

SIMON: No, Zach, that's your thing. I never even liked that.

ZACH: Zach? Who's Zach? It's King…Zachariah to you!

SIMON: Fine. King Zachariah.

ZACH: Today is the day of The Royal Hunt.

SIMON: The what?

ZACH: The Royal Hunt! Once a year we go to the forest outside the castle walls and we have a big competition to see who's the best bow and arrow dude in the whole kingdom. Here, let me show you how it's done. You hold your bow like this. And you pull back the arrow like this. And you wait for something to come by. A deer, or an antelope, or a moose, or a fox, or a wolf, or a bear, or a jaguar, or a cougar, or a mountain lion, or a tiger, or a –

SIMON: We get the picture.

ZACH: And you shoot!

ZACH shoots something ABBY is holding up. She puppeteers its death.

Oh yeeeeah! I got you, sucker. You never stood a chance! Not against the great King Zachariah! What's that? The best shot of the day?! I'm in first place! Woooo! Now you try.

SIMON: I just said I don't want to, Zach.

ZACH: Ah-ah-ah! Who?

SIMON: King Zachariah.

ZACH: Come on – there's something over there.

Again, ABBY creates a target.

Just hold it like this. And pull this back. No, pull harder.

SIMON: I am!

ZACH: Now point and let go.

SIMON does, but…archery fail.

Simon! Come on!

ABBY: Can I try?

ZACH: Excuse me?

ABBY: Can I try to do it?

ZACH: Aren't you that little girl who's always getting Prince Simon to transform?

ABBY: Oh, I uh –

SIMON: Yes. This is my one real friend –

Matt Pilipiak and Cynthia Jimenez-Hicks as the unicorn and Unicorn Killer.

Abby (Cynthia Jimenez-Hicks) offers the king costume to Zach (Drew O'Hara) while Simon (Matt Pilipiak) looks on.

ABBY: Abigail. (*She finds herself a costume piece to take on this role – maybe a cool hunter look.*) I'm his friend, Abigail.

ZACH: Princes aren't allowed to be friends with girls.

ABBY: Who made up that rule?

ZACH: I did. And I'm the king. Girls aren't friends with princes and girls definitely can't shoot a bow and arrow.

ABBY: What? Can't I at least try?

ZACH: No! The Royal Hunt is for boys only.

ABBY: But that's not fair. Girls should be allowed to compete too.

ZACH: Are you arguing with the king?

ABBY: Maybe I am!

ZACH: How dare you, little girl? I am King Zachariah!

ABBY: I don't care! Let me try it.

ZACH: No!

SIMON: Zach, just let her.

ZACH: NO!

A game of keep-away:

ABBY: Just let –

ZACH: Nope.

ABBY: Me –

ZACH: Nope.

ABBY: Try!

SIMON: Hey, Zach! There's something behind you!

ZACH: (*He turns.*) What?

ABBY: It's a mouse!

ZACH: AHHH!

ABBY: (*Snatching the bow and arrow.*) Ha HA!

ZACH: ARGH!

ABBY: Sorry, King. Gotta prove you wrong.

SIMON holds up a target this time. ABBY shoots. It dies.

Ohhhh! First shot! Perfect aim!

SIMON: What's that? Better than the king? She wins the competition? Wooooo! Go, Abigail!

ABBY: I'm the best bow and arrow person in the whole kingdom!

ZACH: (*Snatching back the bow and arrow.*) Nope. Doesn't count. The hunt is over.

ABBY: What?

ZACH: Yeah, the uhh…sun is going down, see? So that means the hunt is over and we have to get back to the castle. Too bad, so sad. Come on, Prince Simon!

SIMON: Wait, Zach, you can't do that to the story.

ZACH: Watch me. (*He creates a huge drawbridge.*) Drawbridge UP!

ABBY: Hey, wait! I'm coming back too.

ZACH: I don't think so. You want a bad guy? I'll show you a bad guy. Say buh-bye to your little friend, Prince Simon.

SIMON: What?

ZACH: Enjoy life alone in the forest, Abigail. DRAWBRIDGE UP!

ABBY: Prince Simon! Wait!

She makes a run for it and grabs onto the raising drawbridge.

SIMON: Grab my hand!

ZACH: No! I banish her from my kingdom! She embarrassed her king.

SIMON: But she's going to fall.

ZACH: Let her. Let her fall into the moat.

SIMON: Not the moat! The moat is full of sea creatures.

ABBY: I can't hold on!

ABBY falls down into the moat.

Noooooo!!!

Splash! SIMON looks down into the moat from the top of the drawbridge.

SIMON: I need to save her.

ZACH: What are you going to do, jump?

SIMON: Uhhhh…

ZACH: From way up here? Aren't you afraid?

SIMON: I uhhhh…

ZACH: You'll never find her down there. The moat is way too deep and way too dark.

SIMON: Dark? That's perfect!

ABBY: (*Calling from below.*) Prince Simon!

SIMON: I wish…

ABBY: Hurry!

SIMON: I wish…

ZACH: Simon, what are you doing?

SIMON: I wish to be a…

ABBY: HELP MEEE!

ZACH: Simon, don't!

SIMON: I WISH TO BE A GIRL!

Beat. Yep, he said it. ABBY takes the dress from the drying rack or clothesline and slips it onto SIMON:

ABBY: And just like that, right there on the drawbridge, Prince Simon magically transforms into…

ABBY & SIMON: A GIRL!

ZACH: Simon, take that off.

SIMON: No.

ZACH: That is Mom's dress.

SIMON: It was in my theatre; I can wear it if I want.

ZACH: Your theatre?

SIMON: It's dark as night – you said so yourself – so that means I can transform.

ZACH: This isn't funny!

SIMON: I have magic powers and there's nothing you can do about it.

ZACH: I'll tell Mom.

SIMON: Yeah? Well, I'll tell her you didn't walk me home from school.

ZACH: Because you left before me! Now Simon, take the dress OFF!

SIMON: NO! I am not Simon anymore! I am not Prince Simon! I am…I am…Princess Simone. YEAH! Princess Simone. And I…I am not afraid of you. Now I have to save my friend. ABIGAIL! I'M COMING!

PRINCESS SIMONE dives into the moat.

ZACH: Cut it out.

ABBY: The sea creatures! They're attacking me!

SIMON: They're no match for Princess Simone. Take that! And that! Hiiii-YA!

ZACH: Stop it!

SIMON: Swim, Abigail!

ABBY: I don't know how!

ZACH has found a big flashlight. He shines the bright light directly on SIMON's face.

ZACH: I said take the dress OFF!

SIMON: Ow! What are you doing?

ZACH: You can only transform in the dark, right? So if there's a light on you, that means your transformation disappears. (*Attempting to remove the dress.*) Don't you get it, Simon? This is why everyone makes fun of you. This is why you're getting bullied so bad! This is why you have no friends! And not only that, the kids in your class will tell everyone else at school you wore a dress in your play and everyone knows you're my brother so then they'll all make fun of me!

SIMON: No! That's not how the play works. You can't just turn a light on and make the dress disappear. My fairy godmother didn't say that. Tell him, Abby.

ABBY: Well… I don't know…

SIMON: What?

ABBY: I mean, technically, he might be right.

SIMON: Abby.

ABBY: You can only transform in the dark. Those are the rules. And…I don't want to get laughed at. I don't want our class to bully me. They don't even know me yet.

SIMON: I told you. This is how they'll get to know you.

ABBY: I'm sorry, Simon, I want to be your friend, but…

SIMON: But what?

ABBY removes the dress from SIMON completely. Beat.

This isn't fun anymore. You can go home now.

ABBY: But what about our play?

SIMON: I don't want to do a play. I'll write my own story. I'll read it in front of the class by myself.

ABBY: But –

SIMON: I said I would be your partner cuz I felt sorry for you cuz no one at school would talk to you. I invited you over to my house, I brought you down to my basement, I told you about my theatre, I showed you my Barbie, and this is what I get?

ABBY: It's just that I'm new and –

SIMON: I transformed. Into My True Self. I wasn't afraid of Zach or King Zachariah or the dark water or the sea creatures. I wasn't afraid of getting laughed at or anything!

ZACH: Simon, calm down.

SIMON: I finally get to be a girl, but you just turn on a flashlight and take it away?

ABBY: Because you can only transform in the dark.

SIMON: You want to be my friend? That's not what a friend would do.

ABBY: I'm just trying to do a good story and get a good mark!

SIMON: NO! You're trying to force me to be a boy like everybody else does!

Pause.

ZACH: Simon, no one is forcing you to be a boy. You are a boy.

SIMON: Get out of my basement. (*To ABBY.*) You can go home now.

ABBY: Oh. (*She takes off her Abigail gear and gets her backpack.*) I'm sorry, I guess I just got…scared.

ABBY exits. Then we hear that magical sound again. Beat.

SIMON: Did you hear that?

ZACH: Hear what?

SIMON: Abby! Wait! Audience, did you hear that?

ZACH: Who are you talking to?

ABBY reenters. The sound again. This time, maybe the light flickers too.

SIMON: There it is again.

ABBY: What?

SIMON: That sound. I don't know what it is, but it sounds like…like magic.

ZACH: Simon, there's no such thing as magic.

SIMON: Abby, can you see them yet?

ABBY: (*Straining to see The Audience.*) No, but I want to.

ZACH: See who?

SIMON: We have to keep going. We have to do the rest of the story.

ABBY: But you just said –

SIMON: I know, I know, but something is happening! What if the spell is real? (*Launching right back into the story.*) So, Audience: in the light from King Zachariah's lantern, Prince Simon turns back into a boy. NOOOO!

ZACH: (*Looking for The Audience.*) There's no one there.

SIMON: Abigail, I was trying to save you!

ABBY: Is the play back on? (*She removes her backpack and puts on her Abigail costume.*)

SIMON: But you betrayed me!

ZACH: Simon, what the heck is going on?

SIMON: I'm escaping to the…The Dark Wood where I can become a girl anytime I want!

ZACH: I don't think so! (*He catches them and resumes his king character.*) A-ha! As for you, little girl, you are outlawed from my kingdom.

ABBY: Outlawed?

ZACH: If you are caught within the castle walls, Abigail, you are dead meat.

ABBY: Nooooo!

ZACH: Now come, Prince Simon, it's time we put an end this transformation business once and for all.

SIMON: What? Where are you taking me?

ZACH: To the tower!

SIMON: The tower?

ZACH: The TOWER OF LIGHT!

SIMON: The Tower of Light? I didn't even know we had this in our kingdom.

ZACH: We only use it for the very worst cases.

SIMON: Cases? Of what?

ZACH: Fairy spells. Those nasty little fairies are always putting spells on people.

SIMON: They are?

ZACH: All the time.

SIMON: Oh. I thought I was special.

ZACH: Special?! Oh please! You're not special. Did you honestly think you were the only one who had the power to transform? Think again. This entire tower is full of freaks just like you.

SIMON: Oh wow! Look at all of them. (*The Audience.*) But why is it called The Tower of Light?

ZACH: Because. In this tower, the lights never, ever go out. Good luck transforming now!

SIMON: But! When do I get out?

ZACH: Out? OUT? The only way to get out is to prove you will never transform again. Guarantee us you won't change into a girl. Once you've done that, you're free to go. But until then, these lights are staying ON!!!

He has created an elaborate tower enclosure for Simon made of Christmas lights and old lamps. He flicks on the lights and exits.

SIMON: Wait! King Zachariah! Don't leave me! (*The door of the tower closes with a loud ka-chunk.*) When I said I wanted to do the rest of the story, this was not what I had in mind. But wait. Audience? Are you really here, in The Tower of Light? Have you been locked up for having transformation powers too? Oh, Audience! People of the tower! We need to get out of here!

SIMON tries to escape to no avail. Then, from the sidelines:

ABBY: The lights!

SIMON: What?

ABBY: The lights. Fairy tales happen way before electricity. Those can't be lights; they're... they're candles!

SIMON: Candles? So I can blow them out and make it dark. And if it's dark... That's perfect!

SIMON starts to blow out the lights, but ZACH appears in a makeshift dragon outfit, doing his best dragon voice.

ZACH: What do you think you're doing?

SIMON: AHHHH! Who are you?

ZACH: The name's… Illumi…nauticus.

SIMON: Illumi-what?

ZACH: Illuminauticus. They call me that because I illuminate the dark. It's my job to keep the lights on.

SIMON: How do you do that?

ZACH: Like this! (*He breathes fire.*) I'm a fire-breathing dragon. Got it?

SIMON: Got it.

ZACH: So you're Prince Simon, eh? Or should I call you Princess Simone?

SIMON: That would be nice.

ZACH: Not gonna happen! I've been sent here by King Zachariah to keep the lights on. And to train you.

SIMON: Train me?

ZACH: To give up the girly act. It's your only chance of freedom. Your only hope of ever having real friends.

SIMON: What? But –

ZACH: Why else do you think Abby took that dress off you?

ABBY: That's not what I –

ZACH: You're outlawed, remember? We can't hear you. (*To SIMON.*) She's not to be trusted, Prince Simon. She told you to blow out these candles and look who showed up! Now: let's see you walk.

SIMON: What?

ZACH: Walk, boy! Let's see you walk! (*SIMON does.*) No, no, no! You walk like a girl!

SIMON: I do?

ZACH: Yes! Now spread those legs.

SIMON: …Like this?

ZACH: And hold those shoulders back!

SIMON: Shoulders back.

ZACH: And stop swinging those hips.

SIMON: Oh, um –

ZACH: Just walk straight ahead.

SIMON: Got it.

ZACH: Chin up! No, chin down! No, chin up. No… chin in. Chin out? Just put your chin in the normal place! Oh jeez – you're gonna need a lot of work. Keep practising, Prince Simon. Practise walking like a man.

SIMON: Sure. I'll practise.

ZACH: And no more blowing out candles. This isn't a birthday cake.

He breathes fire and goes.

ABBY: Simon, I swear, I didn't –

SIMON: I can't hear you. You're outlawed.

Zach (Drew O'Hara) shines a light on Simon (Matt Pilipiak) to remove Mom's dress.

Simon (Matt Pilipiak) in the Tower of Light with Illuminauticus (Drew O'Hara).

ABBY: ...Oh. Then I guess I'm on my own.

A wolf howls.

What was that? No, Abigail, you need to be brave. You need to make things right with your friend. Look – it's snowing! It's winter in The Dark Wood. Okay, Abigail: you need shelter.

SIMON practises in The Tower while ABBY puts her survival skills to use in The Dark Wood. Maybe this is underscored with music.

SIMON: Spread those legs.

ABBY: So you build a fort.

SIMON: Shoulders back!

ABBY: And you make a fire.

SIMON: Stop swinging those hips.

ABBY: And you need something to eat.

SIMON: Just walk straight ahead.

ABBY: So you make a bow and arrow.

SIMON: Chin up.

ABBY: And hunt for your dinner...

SIMON: Chin down.

ABBY: Awww yeah! First shot!

SIMON: Chin in.

ABBY: And chow down.

SIMON: Chin out.

ABBY: Mmm...delicious!

SIMON: Practise walking…

ABBY: And you survive the winter.

SIMON: Like a man.

ABBY: Hey, look! A flower! That must mean spring is here.

This flower discovery could be a bit of magic. And now, ZACH appears out of nowhere. His dragon costume has evolved. Is this something he found upstairs? Hmmm…

ZACH: Spring is here!

SIMON: Zach, don't do that!

ZACH: Zach? Zach who? It's me – Illuminauticus. Looks like you've been practising!

SIMON: Oh. Yeah. (*Shows off the walk.*) How's it look?

ZACH: Meeehhh, still needs some work. But lookee here: I brought you a flower!

SIMON: Purple! My favourite colour!

ZACH: (*Incorrect buzzer sound!*) Purple is a girl colour. Try again. Prince Simon: what's your favourite colour?

SIMON: Uhhh…pink?

ZACH: Even worse!

SIMON: I mean…turquoise?

ZACH: Meeehhh.

SIMON: A nice green?

ZACH: A little closer.

SIMON: Wait! Red?

ZACH: The answer I was looking for was –

ZACH & SIMON: Blue.

ZACH: I would also have accepted grey, black, and navy.

SIMON: Isn't navy just a colour of blue?

ZACH: See!? That's not something boys would say. You gotta work on that.

SIMON: I will.

ZACH: No more purple. No more Barbies. No more Princess Simone.

SIMON: And then can I go? And then will I have friends?

ZACH: We'll see… (*Breathes fire on the flower. It burns to a crisp.*) Mmm! Barbeque!

He exits.

ABBY: Okay, Abigail, you have to save Prince Simon. He thinks you betrayed him! First things first: you need to learn to swim so you can get across that moat.

A training montage in their own separate worlds. Again, there could be music. The theatrical magic continues to grow…

SIMON: Oh, a flower?

ABBY: First: the forward crawl.

SIMON: Oh, no thank you.

ABBY: Then: the backward crawl.

SIMON: I don't like flowers.

ABBY: Then: the butterfly stroke.

SIMON: My favourite colour?

ABBY: Next: train to fight off the sea creatures.

SIMON: I'd have to say my favourite colour is…

ABBY: Take that!

SIMON: Blue.

ABBY: And that!

SIMON: Just regular –

ABBY: Hiii-YA!

SIMON: Plain old –

ABBY: Gotcha!

SIMON: Blue.

ABBY: Now: train to climb the castle wall.

SIMON: Is that a Barbie?

ABBY: (*Rhythmic breathing as she goes through her boot camp.*) Hoo-hoo HA.

SIMON: I don't like Barbies.

ABBY: Hoo-hoo HA.

SIMON: Nope, not me!

ABBY: Hoo-hoo HA.

SIMON: Don't like purple.

ABBY: HOO!

SIMON: Don't like Barbies.

ABBY: HOO!

SIMON: And I am not Princess Simone.

ABBY: HAAA! It's hot! I guess that means summer's here. Prince Simon has been up in that tower for months.

ZACH appears again as Illuminauticus. This time, it's an even bigger, better dragon – definitely not something he found up in the hall closet…

ZACH/ ILLUMINAUTICUS: I'm BAAAA-ACK!

SIMON: AHHH! Illuminauticus, you're…

ZACH/ ILLUMINAUTICUS: I'm what?

SIMON: Nothing, sorry. Just my imagination. There's no such thing as magic.

ZACH/ ILLUMINAUTICUS: Precisely.

SIMON: Is it time for me to get out now?

ZACH/ ILLUMINAUTICUS: You got a bit more work to do before we can be sure you'll never transform again.

SIMON: I won't! I promise! I swear!

ZACH/ ILLUMINAUTICUS: I won't! I promise! I swear! Do you hear yourself? You even sound like a girl. We gotta do something about how you talk. Repeat after me: Hey, did you guys see the hockey game last night?

SIMON: Hey, did you guys see the hockey game last night?

ZACH/
ILLUMINAUTICUS: No, Simon! Use a boy voice.

SIMON: This is just my voice.

ZACH/
ILLUMINAUTICUS: Listen carefully and repeat after me: I'm a boy.

SIMON: I'm a boy.

ZACH/
ILLUMINAUTICUS: I am a boy.

SIMON: I am a boy.

ZACH/
ILLUMINAUTICUS: And I promise to never transform into a girl again.

SIMON: And I promise to never transform into a girl again.

ZACH/
ILLUMINAUTICUS: I am not a girl.

SIMON: I am not a girl.

ZACH/
ILLUMINAUTICUS: I don't like girl stuff.

SIMON: I don't like girl stuff.

ZACH/
ILLUMINAUTICUS: I am not friends with girls.

SIMON: I am not friends with girls.

ZACH/
ILLUMINAUTICUS: I'm a regular prince.

SIMON: I'm a regular prince.

ZACH/
ILLUMINAUTICUS: A normal prince.

SIMON: A normal prince.

ZACH/
ILLUMINAUTICUS: A regular, normal prince who only wants to be a boy.

SIMON: A regular, normal prince who only wants to be a boy.

ZACH/
ILLUMINAUTICUS: Sounding pretty good.

SIMON: Sounding pretty good.

ZACH/
ILLUMINAUTICUS: No, you can stop repeating after me now.

SIMON: No, you can stop repeating after me now.

ZACH/
ILLUMINAUTICUS: Simon! That's enough.

SIMON: Simon! That's – Oh right.

ZACH/
ILLUMINAUTICUS: Keep working on that. I'll check back in.

SIMON: And then can I go? If I sound like a boy, will you let me out?

ZACH/
ILLUMINAUTICUS: I'll see what the king thinks.

SIMON: Cool. Thanks, man.

ZACH/
ILLUMINAUTICUS: Nice, man. Nice.

ZACH goes. Once more, music and montage.

ABBY: Nice! Today's the day. Operation: Rescue Prince Simon.

SIMON: Keep practising.

ABBY: I'm at the moat! Forward crawl...

SIMON: I'm a boy.

ABBY: Backward crawl...

SIMON: I'm a boy.

ABBY: Ahhh! Sea creatures! Hiiii-YA!

SIMON: I am a boy.

ABBY: Take that!

SIMON: And I promise to never transform into a girl again.

ABBY: And that!

SIMON: And I promise to never transform into a girl again.

ABBY: See ya, sea creatures! Eat my dust.

SIMON: And I promise to never transform into a girl again.

ABBY: Next: climb the castle wall.

SIMON: I am not a girl.

ABBY: Hoo-hoo HA!

SIMON: I am not a girl.

ABBY: Hoo-hoo HA!

SIMON: I am not a girl!

ABBY: Hoo-hoo YAAA! I made it inside the kingdom!

SIMON: I don't like girl stuff.

ABBY: But I need to make sure no one sees me.

SIMON: I don't like girl stuff.

ABBY: Cuz if I get caught within the castle walls...

SIMON: I don't like girl stuff.

ZACH appears in ABBY's scene as King Zachariah. The music cuts out.

ZACH: You are DEAD MEAT!

ABBY: Oh no! King Zachariah!

ZACH: What do you think you're doing here, Abigail?

ABBY: I'm here to rescue Prince Simon.

ZACH: You wish! There's only one way he can be set free: prove he'll never become a girl again!

ABBY: And when will that be?

ZACH: I wouldn't hold my breath. As for you, Abigail... (*He pulls out his bow and arrow.*)

ABBY: You call that a bow and arrow? (*She pulls out hers. It's way bigger.*) THIS is a bow and arrow!

ZACH: What the – ?! (*He puts his hands up.*)

ABBY: You're gonna go riiiight back here. Oh! And just in case... (*She grabs the mermaid costume from earlier.*) This'll teach you not to mess with a girl.

ABBY leads ZACH off at arrow-point. SIMON is alone on stage, a shadow of his former self.

SIMON: I am not friends with girls. I am just a regular prince. A normal prince. A regular, normal prince who only wants to be a boy. I am not a girl… I am not a girl…

Knock, knock, knock.

Who's there?

ABBY: (*Doing her best king voice from off.*) Uhhh…it's me. The king. King Zachariah.

SIMON: Come in.

ABBY enters the tower wearing the king's crown and cape.

ABBY: Prince Simon?

SIMON: Hello, King Zachariah. Are you here to let me out?

ABBY: (*In her own voice.*) Yeah, I –

SIMON: I promise I won't ever transform again.

ABBY: What?

SIMON: I am a boy. This is how I walk. This is how I talk. My favourite colour is blue.

ABBY: Simon, it's me. It's Abigail. (*She reveals herself.*)

SIMON: Abigail?

ABBY: What is wrong with you? You're not acting like yourself.

SIMON: This is me now. A normal prince. Shoulders back!

ABBY: Simon, stop it! I'm here to get you out. I made a bow and arrow. I fought the sea creatures, I climbed the wall –

SIMON: But – those are boy things.

ABBY: What?

SIMON: Bow and arrow, fighting, and climbing. Those are boy things.

ABBY: There's no such thing as boy things and girl things. You know that! Now come on.

SIMON: I'm getting out on my own.

ABBY: No, you're not! King Zachariah and Illuminauticus – they're never letting you out of here!

SIMON: Yes, they are! I just need to show them I'm a regular prince.

ABBY: But you're not regular! You can transform. You jumped from the drawbridge, remember? You saved me from drowning. Princess Simone wasn't afraid. That is Your True Self. Your True Self is A GIRL!

SIMON: I AM NOT A GIRL!

ABBY: You used to think being a girl was amazing.

SIMON: If it's so amazing, why are you dressed like that? Why are you disguised as the king?

ABBY: Because I'm trying to save you!

SIMON: No, you're trying to trick me! Trick me into being your friend like you did before! Illuminauticus!

ABBY: What are you doing?

SIMON: Get in here!

ABBY: Simon, no.

SIMON: Illuminauticus!

ILLUMINAUTICUS appears. Now, it is a full-blown life-size dragon – as big and terrifying as you can make it.

ILLUMINAUTICUS: Yes, Prince?

SIMON: This is not the king. This is Abigail – pretending to be something she's not.

ABBY: Nooo!

She tries to escape, but ILLUMINAUTICUS stops her.

ILLUMINAUTICUS: Nice try, Abigail. You know what we do to girls like you?

ABBY: Lock me in the tower?

ILLUMINAUTICUS: You wish! Girls like you get special treatment. You're gonna BURN!

He breathes fire. She can't escape.

ABBY: Nooo!!!

ILLUMINAUTICUS: This is what you get for telling Prince Simon His True Self is a girl.

ABBY: Simon, help me.

ILLUMINAUTICUS: Trying to convince him he's something he's not.

ABBY: Simon!

ILLUMINAUTICUS: This is what you get for not knowing your place!

ABBY: I'm here to make things right. I'm here to be your friend.

SIMON: I am not friends with girls.

ABBY: But you're friends with me! Or I want you to be. You're the only one in our class who's nice to me. It wasn't Ms. da Silva's idea for you to be my partner. I asked her if I could work with you.

SIMON: What?

ABBY: I asked to do the fairy tale with you so I could be your friend. I need a friend, Simon. And so do you.

SIMON: I – I am not friends with…

ILLUMINAUTICUS: That's right.

SIMON: I am not friends with…

ABBY: Please!

ILLUMINAUTICUS: Don't listen to her!

SIMON: I am not…

Beat. Simon looks to The Audience.

I wish.

The magic sound.

ILLUMINAUTICUS: You what?

SIMON: There's too much light in here. I need to get these candles out. (*Starts to blow.*)

ILLUMINAUTICUS: What do you think you're doing? (*FIRE!*)

SIMON & ABBY: AHHHHH!!!!

ILLUMINAUTICUS: Ohhhh! Are you afraid of me?

SIMON: Yes! Yes, I am afraid of you! I'm afraid of myself! I'm afraid of everything! That's why I need to – (*He blows on the candles.*) Abigail, help me!

ILLUMINAUTICUS: It will never work. Your breath is no match for my fire.

SIMON: The other people! The other people in the tower!

ABBY: What?

SIMON: Audience! We need your help!

ILLUMINAUTICUS: What is going on?

SIMON: I need you to blow out these candles and make it dark. (*Blowing on the lights.*) I wish…

ABBY: Ahhh! I see them!

SIMON: I wish!

ILLUMINAUTICUS: Don't even think about it.

He catches SIMON.

SIMON: Ahh!

ABBY: Yes, blow, Audience! BLOW!

SIMON: I wish to be…

ABBY: It's working! It's dark!

SIMON: MY TRUE SELF!!!

With this, ILLUMINAUTICUS yanks SIMON out of the Tower of Light. Or SIMON magically disappears from ILLUMINAUTICUS's grasp.

Darkness. Then fire. Then light.

And magic…

ABBY: Simon?

ILLUMINAUTICUS: What the – Where did he go?

ABBY: ...Hello?

Now, PRINCESS SIMONE appears in SIMON's place, wearing a resplendent fairy tale gown. There's no way this dress is from this basement. No way it's from this house. It is otherworldly, and the purplest shade of purple.

ILLUMINAUTICUS: Who are you?

SIMON(E): I am Princess Simone.

ILLUMINAUTICUS: No! You're...you're Prince Simon.

SIMON(E): Not anymore. This is My True Self.

ILLUMINAUTICUS: But that's...disgusting. You were training so hard. It was going so well! Why would you throw all that away?

SIMON(E): Because that's not real! That's not who I am!

ILLUMINAUTICUS: You're only eight years old. How would you know who you are?

SIMON(E): I just know.

ILLUMINAUTICUS: One breath of fire and I could burn you and your little friend to a crisp. Aren't you afraid of that?

SIMON(E): ...No.

ILLUMINAUTICUS breathes fire.

ABBY: Uhhh, Simon?!

SIMON(E): Simone. I am not afraid of you, Illuminauticus. You think you're so tough but it's YOU who's afraid.

ILLUMINAUTICUS: What?!

SIMON(E): You're afraid of anything that's different – you and King Zachariah. You're afraid of boys with Barbies; boys who like purple and wear dresses. Afraid of girls dressed as boys who can swim and climb and fight. And when you get afraid, you get mean and awful. And you are my brother, Zach; you're my big brother and you're supposed to stand up for me and love me and this is My True Self and I AM NOT AFRAID OF YOU!

ZACH has appeared during this. If possible, ILLUMINAUTICUS is also still present.

ZACH: Simon, just –

SIMON(E): NOW LET! US! GO!

ZACH: What?

SIMON(E): Let us go. Me and Abigail and all the people in the Tower of Light. We are not afraid of you.

ZACH: Uh, okay…Your Majesty. Here. You can go.

ZACH releases them from the tower and exits. SIMONE and ABIGAIL could even break the fourth wall here and go into The Audience.

SIMON(E): And Princess Simone…and Abigail…and all the others from the Tower of Light come into the courtyard. It's the middle of the night – dark, dark, dark – and we all transform…and transform and transform into whatever we wish. Into…Our True Selves.

ABBY: And Illuminauticus disappears –

SIMON(E): And the Tower of Light crumbles to the ground.

ABBY: And the Fairy Godmother watches from high in the sky and says, "You did it! You found Your True Selves!"

SIMON(E): But wait! What about King Zachariah?

ABBY: Oh, I wouldn't worry about him. Hey, King Zachariah! Come on out here and show us how it looks!

ABBY raises her bow and arrow as ZACH enters in the mermaid costume. SIMON(E) cracks up.

ZACH: What are you laughing at?

SIMON(E): You!

ZACH: Simon! It's not nice to laugh at people.

SIMON(E): Sorry, it's just – That is definitely not Your True Self.

ZACH: Guess not. (*To ABBY.*) Can I please take this off now? (*She lowers her weapon.*) Thank you.

ABBY: Did all that actually just happen? Was that just our imaginations? Cuz that was amazing! This is going to be the best story in our whole class. Ms. da Silva is going to give us perfect; more than perfect; one hundred and ten percent. Zach, the presentations are tomorrow right after lunch. You have to come to our class and do the play with us.

ZACH: I'm not doing all that in front of your class!

ABBY: Why not?

SIMON(E): You afraid?

ZACH: No. Fine, I'll get a note and come down when it's time.

ABBY: So is that it? Is that the end of our fairy tale? And they all lived happily ever –

SIMON(E): Wait! It's not happily ever after. Because morning comes, and the sun begins to rise, and the dark –

ABBY: Becomes light.

SIMON(E): And the transformations disappear. Until it's dark again, Prince Simon is afraid.

ZACH: NO! Simon, no. You don't have to change back. Even in the light, even upstairs, or outside, or at school, I don't... I don't want you to be afraid.

From upstairs, we hear the door and –

MOM: Hello! We're home from work!

DAD: Simon? Zach? Where are you boys?

ZACH: We're in the basement!

ABBY: Oh my gosh, what time is it? I gotta go. My mom's probably wondering where I am. Thanks for having me over...partner. Friend. Simone. (*She hands Barbie over.*) Hey, that dress is really, really fancy. Was that in your costume box?

SIMON(E): No, I don't know where this came from.

ABBY: Well, you look...amazing. See ya tomorrow!

ABBY exits.

ZACH: Seriously though. Where the heck is that from?

SIMON(E): I have no idea.

Abigail (Cynthia Jimenez-Hicks) and Princess Simone (Matt Pilipiak) come face-to-face with Illuminauticus.

Simone (Matt Pilipiak) and Barbie share a moment with The Audience.

The magic sound again. SIMON(E) looks at the Barbie in their hand. ZACH looks at it too.

ZACH: So if this is like…Your True Self and everything, does that mean you're gonna be a girl all the time? Like, instead of being my brother, are you my sister now or something?

SIMON(E): Um, I don't really know. Maybe? Maybe not.

ZACH: Abby's right, you know. You look…okay in purple.

On the stairs, ZACH looks at The Audience. He still can't see them.

Hey – who the heck is out there?

SIMON(E): Never mind.

ZACH exits. SIMONE is alone, in the dress, with the Barbie, and The Audience.

SIMONE: Ohhhhh, Audience! That was… And this is… And you – all of you are… Thank you for your help with the candles. Now that you're free, be Your True Selves, okay? I will if you will. (*They smile. On the way out –*) Mom? Dad! I have something to show you!

And SIMONE goes upstairs.

Darkness and magic and music and light. And because it's a fairy tale…dancing!

The end.